The Honey Hunters

Adapted from a story by Geraldine Elliot
Illustrated by Chantal Stewart

CELEBRATION PRESS
Pearson Learning Group

Once upon a time all the wild animals were the greatest of friends. And, as it happened, they all loved honey.

The little gray honeyguide knew the best places to find honey.

"Che, che! Cheka, cheka, che!" the bird would cry. "If you want honey, follow me!"

One day a boy was walking by the lake when he heard the honeyguide's song.

"I'd like some honey," he said. "I'll follow you."

And so the boy and the honeyguide set off together through the forest.

6

Very soon they met a rooster.

"Che, che! Cheka, cheka, che!" sang the honeyguide. "If you want honey, follow me!"

"I'd like some honey," said the rooster, fluffing up his tail feathers. "I'll follow you."

And so the rooster joined the boy as he followed the honeyguide through the forest.

They had not gone far when they saw a bush cat.

"Che, che! Cheka, cheka, che!" sang the honeyguide. "If you want honey, follow me!"

"I'd like some honey," said the bush cat, dropping from the tree. "I'll follow you."

So the honeyguide and the boy and the rooster and the bush cat set off together.

By and by they
met an antelope …

and then a leopard …

and then a zebra …

and then a lion …

"Che, che! Cheka, cheka, che!" the honeyguide sang to each of the animals. "If you want honey, follow me!"

So the antelope and the leopard, the zebra and the lion, joined the boy and the rooster and the bush cat as they followed the honeyguide through the forest.

Pretty soon the animals met an elephant.

"Where are you all going, my friends?" he asked.

"To find some honey," replied the boy.

"Che, che! Cheka, cheka, che!" sang the honeyguide. "If you want honey, follow me!"

So the elephant joined the procession of animals going in search of honey.

In a short while, the honeyguide stopped.

"Che, che! Cheka, cheka, che!" he sang again.
"If you want honey, look in this tree!"

Then the boy took a beautiful honeycomb from the bees' nest and broke it into four pieces.

The first he gave to the rooster and the bush cat.

The second he gave to the antelope and the leopard.

The third he gave to the zebra and the lion.

And the fourth he kept for himself and the elephant.

Then all the animals began to eat . . .

The rooster pecked his end of the honeycomb, and the bush cat licked his.

Then the bush cat hissed at the rooster, and the rooster scratched the bush cat.

The antelope nibbled her end of the honeycomb, and the leopard gulped his.

Then the leopard clawed the antelope, and the antelope kicked the leopard.

The zebra chewed her end of the honeycomb, and the lion tore off a big chunk.

Then the lion leapt upon the zebra, and the zebra bit the lion with her sharp teeth.

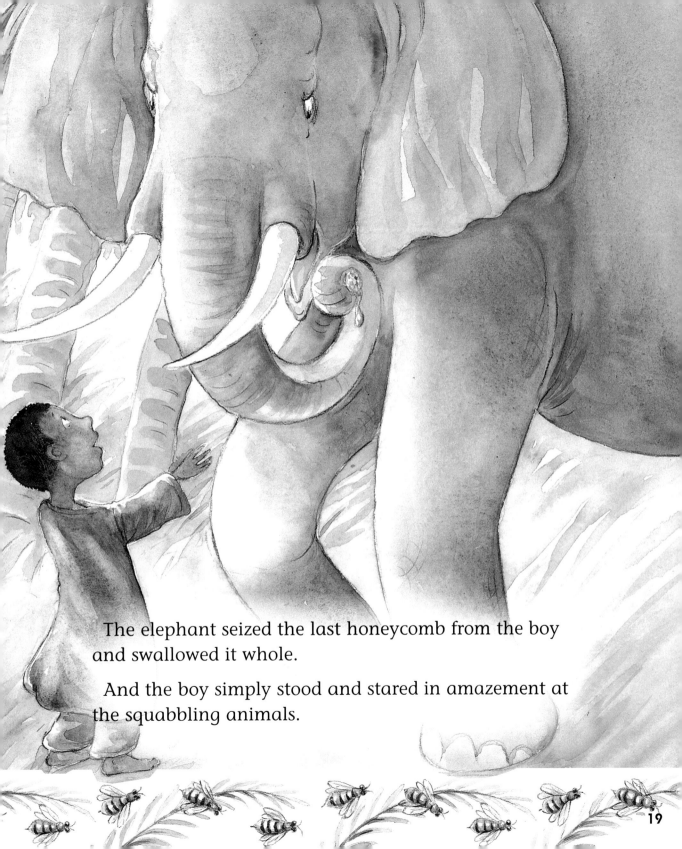

The elephant seized the last honeycomb from the boy and swallowed it whole.

And the boy simply stood and stared in amazement at the squabbling animals.

"Stop! Stop!" cried the boy in alarm. "Don't fight! You have never quarreled with each other before!"

But the animals refused to listen.

Then the boy grew very angry. "Stop fighting at once!" he shouted in a voice like thunder.

At this, the animals fell silent.

Then the elephant spoke. "The damage is done," he said sadly. "We can never be friends again. From now on we shall be enemies: the rooster and the bush cat, the antelope and the leopard, the zebra and the lion, and myself and man."

Then all the animals turned and disappeared into the bush. Only the boy and the honeyguide remained.

"Che, che! Cheka, cheka, che!" sang the honeyguide. "If you want honey, follow me."

Still singing his happy song, the little bird flew off into the bush. And—after a moment's pause—his friend followed.